BATMAN
SUPERMAN

VOLUME 1 CROSS WORLD

BATMAN/ SUPERMAN

VOLUME 1
CROSS WORLD

GREG **PAK** writer

JAE **LEE** PAULO **SIQUEIRA** BEN **OLIVER**
YILDIRAY **CINAR** NETHO **DIAZ** artists

JUNE **CHUNG** DANIEL **BROWN** HI-FI
MATT **YACKEY** JOHN **KALISZ** colorists

ROB **LEIGH** DEZI **SIENTY** letterers

JAE **LEE** with JUNE **CHUNG**
collection cover artists

BATMAN created by BOB **KANE**
SUPERMAN created by JERRY **SIEGEL** & JOE **SHUSTER**
By special arrangement with the Jerry Siegel family

EDDIE BERGANZA Editor – Original Series RICKEY PURDIN Associate Editor – Original Series
ANTHONY MARQUES Assistant Editor – Original Series ROBIN WILDMAN Editor ROBBIN BROSTERMAN Design Director – Books
ROBBIE BIEDERMAN Publication Design

BOB HARAS Senior VP – Editor-in-Chief, DC Comics

DIANE NELSON President DAN DIDIO and JIM LEE Co-Publishers GEOFF JOHNS Chief Creative Officer
JOHN ROOD Executive VP – Sales, Marketing and Business Development AMY GENKINS Senior VP – Business and Legal Affairs
NAIRI GARDINER Senior VP – Finance JEFF BOISON VP – Publishing Planning
MARK CHIARELLO VP – Art Direction and Design JOHN CUNNINGHAM VP – Marketing
TERRI CUNNINGHAM VP – Editorial Administration ALISON GILL Senior VP – Manufacturing and Operations
HANK KANALZ Senior VP – Vertigo and Integrated Publishing JAY KOGAN VP – Business and Legal Affairs, Publishing
JACK MAHAN VP – Business Affairs, Talent NICK NAPOLITANO VP – Manufacturing Administration
SUE POHJA VP – Book Sales COURTNEY SIMMONS Senior VP – Publicity BOB WAYNE Senior VP – Sales

BATMAN/SUPERMAN VOLUME 1: CROSS WORLD

DC Comics, 1700 Broadway, New York, NY 10019
A Warner Bros. Entertainment Company.
Printed by RR Donnelley, Salem, VA, USA. 3/28/14. First Printing.

HC ISBN: 978-1-4012-4509-2
SC ISBN: 978-1-4012-4934-2

Library of Congress Cataloging-in-Publication Data

Pak, Greg, author.
Batman/Superman. Volume 1, Cross World / Greg Pak ; illustrated by Jae Lee.
pages cm. — (The New 52!)
Summary: "The Dark Knight and the Man of Steel are close friends in the modern day—but the two weren't always such close allies.
Discover how two of the World's Finest Super Heroes met for the first time in the New 52, and the mysterious adventure that takes them
to a whole new world-the world of Earth 2! The heroes of the main DC Universe meet their Earth 2 counterparts for the first time!
Collects Batman/Superman #1-4 and Justice League #23.1: Darkseid"— Provided by publisher.
Batman created by Bob Kane.
Superman created by Jerry Siegel and Joe Shuster.
ISBN 978-1-4012-4509-2 (hardback)
1. Graphic novels. I. Lee, Jae, 1972- illustrator. II. Title. III. Title: Cross World.
PN6728.B36P34 2014
741.5'973—dc23
2014000327

SUSTAINABLE FORESTRY INITIATIVE

Certified Chain of Custody
At Least 20% Certified Forest Content
www.sfiprogram.org
SFI-01042
APPLIES TO TEXT STOCK ONLY

GREG PAK writer JAE LEE BEN OLIVER artists JUNE CHUNG DANIEL BROWN colorists cover by JAE LEE with JUNE CHUNG

My father was a doctor.

He saw hundreds of people cut open and shot apart.

He knew how insane and cruel this world is.

But he promised to always keep me safe.

Easier said than done.

AAAAGH!

But this kid's tougher than I was.

He's thinking about it now.

Seconds away from changing everything.

DO IT.

Heh.

DIDN'T EXPECT *BRUCE WAYNE* TO BE SO *STREET SMART.*

Whoa. He just MADE me. Who IS this guy?

BRUCE WAYNE? I LOOK LIKE A *BILLIONAIRE* TO YOU?

How long's he been watching? What's he seen?

CLARK KENT. *METROPOLIS DAILY STAR.*

Wayne's playing dumb. I guess I can understand.

He smells like a strip club. Perfume. Smoke. Sweat. Maybe a little blood. Someone punched him in the face not too long ago.

FUN NIGHT, huh?

OKAY. YOU CAUGHT ME. RICH BOY SLUMMING ON THE EAST END. HOW MUCH FOR YOU TO WALK AWAY AND PRETEND THIS NEVER--

I DON'T WRITE THE *GOSSIP COLUMN,* MR. WAYNE.

I'M JUST CURIOUS IF YOU HAVE ANY COMMENT ABOUT *THESE.*

THREE *WAYNE ENTERPRISES* EMPLOYEES HAVE BEEN *MURDERED* IN *METROPOLIS* IN THE LAST EIGHT HOURS.

ANY IDEA WHAT THIS MIGHT BE ABOUT?

He's big.

But I'm fast--

--and he doesn't seem to be terribly bright.

Then again, maybe he doesn't have to be.

He's snapping the titanium bones of those bots like carrots.

And as it turns out, he's pretty fast, too.

UNGH!

That wasn't even a punch.

If he sneezes, I'm dead.

SO YOUNG.

SO ANGRY.

SO RAW.

SO PERFECT.

Huh.
WHERE'D THEY GO?

OW.
METROPOLIS?

WHAT THE HELL AM I DOING IN *THIS* DUMP?

GREG PAK writer   JAE LEE artist   JUNE CHUNG colorist   cover by JAE LEE with JUNE CHUNG

BOOOOOM

WHAT THE HELL--

Wayne Manor?

This is a disaster. Someone teleported me here. Someone knows...

...someone knows Batman is Bruce Wayne.

WELCOME HOME, SIR.

Catwoman just tried to kill me in Metropolis...

ALFRED! MEET ME IN THE INFIRMARY!

...but she doesn't teleport people, the last time I checked.

IT'S ALFRED'S *NIGHT OFF,* DARLING.

I KIND OF LIKE IT.

None of this makes sense.

And then...

...all of a sudden...

...it almost does.

That's... a wedding photo.

WHAT NEXT, HUSBAND?

But we're not married...

...in my world.

This is insane.

My parents are dead.

I sat by my father's side in the *hospice*...

...listening so hard, his last breath sounded like a *hurricane*.

And then the *silence* that followed nearly broke my eardrums.

I know this isn't real. This *can't* be real. This can't—

DAD...

STAY BACK.

DAD, WAIT—

I'M NOT YOUR FATHER.

MY BOY WOULD NEVER BEAT HIS *BEST FRIEND SENSELESS* THE WAY YOU JUST DID.

WHAT? I—

He's talking about the bat-thing that attacked me.

He's got it all mixed up. I want to *explain*. But then—

JUST... STAY BACK.

Shame. Sharp and searing, like a razor slicing upwards from my belly to my throat.

And then—

Anger.

WHAT KIND OF TRICK IS THIS?

I DON'T--

YOU *ATTACKED* ME IN *METROPOLIS!*

AND NOW YOU TELEPORT ME *HERE* AND SHOW ME THIS--

--THIS *LIE!*

WHAT DO YOU *WANT* FROM ME?

NOTHING.

I DIDN'T SET THIS UP, AND I DON'T KNOW WHO *DID.*

BUT I THINK I'M STARTING TO UNDERSTAND WHAT'S GOING--

THIS ONE'S A BIT TOO CLEVER.

BOOOM

NO! YOU CAN'T RUN--

SHAKOOOOM

WHAT THE DEVIL--

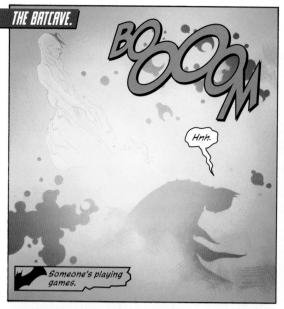

BOOOOOM

Hnh.

Someone's playing games.

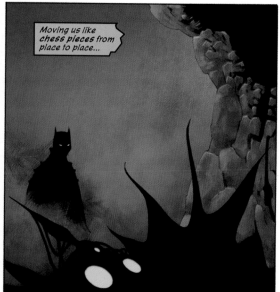

Moving us like *chess pieces* from place to place...

...or *world to world*...

MY GOD.

I've got a double, too.

HA!

YOU! STOP!

I sound like an idiot.

This thing can apparently cross dimensions or bend reality...

...and I'm yelling at it like a beat cop.

I SAID STOP!

But this is my home.

And my heart's in my throat.

What if my double is as crazy as *Clark's*?

What if...

What if...

WHAT STORY DID I ASK MY FATHER TO READ ME EVERY NIGHT FOR A MONTH WHEN I WAS FIVE YEARS OLD?

"THE VELDT." RAY BRADBURY.

HE'S *YOU*, DARLING. JUST YOUNGER.

TIME TRAVEL? OR ALTERNATE UNIVERSE?

I VOTE FOR *MAGIC*.

COULD BE ANY OF THEM...

...BUT THERE WAS A *WOMAN* HERE. I SAW A GHOSTLY KIND OF *PRESENCE*...

IF SHE WERE STILL HERE, THE MANSION'S ALARMS WOULD HAVE ALERTED ME.

THERE'S *ANOTHER* PROBLEM.

WHEN I WAS TELEPORTED HERE FROM MY WORLD, I WAS FIGHTING SOME KIND OF *VILLAIN*. HE WORE *RED AND BLUE*. AND HE WAS MORE *POWERFUL* THAN ANY HUMAN EVER SHOULD BE.

HE'S THE *MOST DANGEROUS PERSON* I'VE EVER SEEN. AND IF HE MADE IT OVER...

DON'T WORRY. I'VE GOT A *FRIEND* TAKING CARE OF IT.

Heh.

"...you haven't seen anything yet."

HELLO, CLARKS.

LOIS LANE. I DON'T RECALL SENDING OUT A PRESS ADVISORY...

COME ON, YOU SHOULD KNOW BY NOW YOU CAN'T KEEP ANY SECRETS FROM ME.

THIS IS ALL OFF THE RECORD--

FINE, FINE...

...I JUST WANTED TO SEE WHAT AN ALTERNATE-WORLD VERSION OF MY HUSBAND LOOKS LIKE.

YOUR... HUSBAND?

SURPRISED?

AH... NO. IT'S JUST...

...I MEAN, YES.

IN MY WORLD, WE'RE JUST FRIENDS.

Hmp. WELL. YOUR LOSS.

WHO ARE YOU DATING, THEN?

DATING? Uh. NO ONE AT THE--

NNNNEEEIGGH!

GREG PAK writer   JAE LEE & YILDIRAY CINAR artists   JUNE CHUNG, MATT YACKEY & JOHN KALISZ colorists   cover by JAE LEE with JUNE CHUNG

THE BOY'S NAME IS **CLARK KENT**.

A FEW MONTHS AGO, HE PUT ON A **CAPE** AND STARTED FIGHTING **CRIME**.

HE THOUGHT **THAT** WAS PRETTY CRAZY...

...BUT NOW HE'S ON A **PARALLEL WORLD** WATCHING A BATTLE BETWEEN **GODDESSES**.

DEMON!

HE'S COMPLETELY OUT OF HIS DEPTH.

BUT BACK HOME, THEY CALL HIM **SUPERMAN**. SO--

STAND BACK, MA'AM! I'LL TAKE CARE--

"MA'AM"?

SPLIT SCREEN

IN THE MEANTIME, I HAVE MY *OWN* PROBLEMS TO ATTEND TO.

THE *LASSO OF TRUTH* COMPELS YOU!

MAGIC *ROPE?* Hnh.

WHO ARE YOU AND WHAT HAVE YOU COME FOR?

I DIDN'T PLAN TO *REVEAL* MYSELF SO *SOON...*

AAAAAAGH!

...BUT MAYBE IT'S TIME TO STIR THE POT.

I SEE YOU, *KAIYO...*

...*CHAOS BRINGER...*

...AND I AM *COMING.*

WHOA.

HA. *YOUNG* CLARK JUST HEARD *OLD* CLARK'S *HEART* SKIP.

WHO'S... WHO'S THE *MONSTER?*

I HAVE NO IDEA.

AND NOW, FOR THE *FIRST* TIME...

...HE'S *SCARED.*

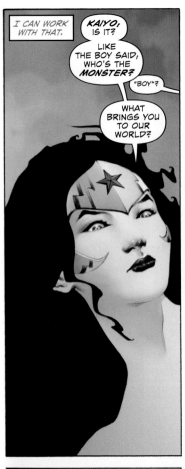

I CAN WORK WITH THAT.

KAIYO, IS IT? LIKE THE BOY SAID, WHO'S THE MONSTER?

"BOY"?

WHAT BRINGS YOU TO OUR WORLD?

LISTEN...

YOUR BATMAN.

HE HAS A SECRET.

HENCE THE MASK. WE KNOW.

NO.

HE'S BEEN HIDING YOUR WORLD'S MOST DANGEROUS WEAPON.

I THOUGHT THAT WAS YOU.

Hm.

DOUBT. SUCH A BEAUTIFUL THING.

I'VE SEEN THAT CRYSTAL. YOUR...BATMAN USED IT AGAINST ME.

AND NOW A LITTLE RIGHTEOUS ANGER.

I KNOCKED IT AWAY FROM HIM--

WHAT-- HOLD, DEMON!

I'LL LET THEM TAKE IT FROM HERE.

HA HA HA!

HEY! COME BACK--

SO YOU LAST SAW THAT CRYSTAL IN SMALLVILLE?

YES, BUT--

AHA. I SEE IT.

YOU *SEE* IT?

BUT THAT'S *HUNDREDS* OF MILES AWAY. HOW COULD YOU--

SHOOOOM

SO WHEN I GROW UP, I'LL BE A JERK?

CUT HIM SOME SLACK, KID.

YOU WOULDN'T HAVE A LOT OF TIME FOR SMALL TALK, EITHER...

"...IF YOU'D JUST FOUND OUT YOU'D BEEN *BETRAYED* BY YOUR *BEST FRIEND.*"

DAMMIT, BRUCE...

...still surprising me...

I'd never seen a car that big...

YOU NEED SOME HELP, MISTER?

OH, NO. NO, THANK YOU, YOUNG MAN.

I'VE FIGURED IT OUT. ALL IT'LL TAKE NOW IS A LITTLE TIME.

...or a kid that...sad.

HI.

HEY.

I wasn't exactly what you'd call an extrovert, myself. Too many secrets.

So I don't know why...

...but the words fell out of my mouth before I even thought them.

WANNA PLAY?

NOT A BAD IDEA, MASTER BRUCE.

So let's see what's up your sleeve today, Bruce.

BE CAREFUL.

YOUR BATMAN NEARLY KILLED ME WITH THAT.

KRYPTONITE?

NO, WONDER WOMAN. IT'S A *MAGNIFIER* OF SOME KIND. IT *AMPLIFIED* AND *FOCUSED* THE RADIATION CREATED BY A MUCH SMALLER BIT OF KRYPTONITE.

I HAVEN'T ACTUALLY SEEN THIS SUBSTANCE BEFORE...

AHA.

AHA?

GOTHAM'S THE *OTHER* WAY, CLARK!

WE'RE NOT *GOING* TO GOTHAM.

BUT--

YOU CAN SEE IT, CAN'T YOU, CLARK?

This older me's testing me. Annoying.

THE CRYSTAL HAS A STRUCTURE LIKE NOTHING ELSE ON THE PLANET.

NOW THAT YOU KNOW WHAT TO *LOOK* FOR, JUST FILTER THE REST OUT...

And then I see.

MY GOD...

WHAT?

"MILES AWAY--SOME KIND OF *BUNKER*. WHO IS IT, THE *ARMY?*"

"NO, CLARK. PAY ATTENTION. IF YOU *LISTEN*, YOU'LL HEAR THE *NSA* AGENTS COMMUNICATING.

"THIS IS A SECRET UNIT, DIRECTLY UNDER THE SUPERVISION OF THE PRESIDENT.

"AND IF YOU LOOK A LITTLE HARDER...

"...YOU'LL SEE WHAT THEY'RE TRYING SO HARD TO HIDE."

SO BRUCE BETRAYED YOU AFTER ALL?

NO, DIANA, IT'S NOT LIKE THAT.

YEARS AGO, I TOLD HIM TO *PREPARE*...

...IN CASE SOMETHING EVER *HAPPENED* TO ME. IN CASE I LOST *CONTROL*.

SOMEONE NEEDED TO BE ABLE TO STOP ME.

AND WHO STOPS THE *BAT?*

JONATHAN... I HAVE A CONFESSION TO MAKE.

Uh-oh. SOUNDS SERIOUS.

I COULD HAVE FIXED THE CAR BY NOW.

BUT IT'S BEEN SO LONG... I WANTED TO GIVE BRUCE A CHANCE...

...A CHANCE TO PLAY.

Hm.

YOU KNOW, IT MIGHT NOT BE SO OBVIOUS, ALFRED...

"...BUT I'VE BEEN WATCHING OUT FOR A PRETTY LONELY KID, TOO."

GOSH. BEAUTIFUL NIGHT, *huh?*

CRACK

HEY! WHAT'S THE BIG IDEA?

YOU'RE *STRONGER* THAN YOU LET ON.

STRONGER THAN *ANYBODY.*

WHY DO YOU *HIDE* IT?

YOU KNOW...

...SOMETIMES I FEEL LIKE I DON'T REALLY BELONG HERE.

THAT IF PEOPLE REALLY KNEW ME...

...THEY'D BE *SCARED* OF ME.

THAT... SOUNDS PRETTY AWESOME.

HA.

For twenty years, Bruce has been my *best friend...*

...*because he was never scared.*

THUMP

THUNK

FFFFT

YOU'RE INSANE!

Psh. YOU'RE THE **BILLIONAIRE** IN THE **BAT COSTUME.**

YOU FIGURE THAT OUT **YOURSELF** OR DID YOUR **DOUBLE** HAVE TO TELL YOU?

THEY TALKED ABOUT **GOTHAM,** CALLED YOU **BRUCE.** I PUT IT TOGETHER.

RIGHT. INTREPID REPORTER **CLARK KENT.**

HUMAN AFTER ALL.

I WOULDN'T GO **THAT** FAR.

SKRAAKKK

HA.

THIS HAS ALL BEEN STRANGE AND KIND OF *FUN*, HASN'T IT?

BUT NOW IT'S TIME TO BE SERIOUS.

WE GREW UP ON DIFFERENT WORLDS IN DIFFERENT WAYS.

BUT I KNOW YOU, BRUCE. AND I *DEFINITELY* KNOW YOU, CLARK.

YOU'RE WEARING THOSE CAPES BECAUSE YOU WANT TO *HELP* PEOPLE. AND THAT'S EXACTLY WHAT WE'RE GOING TO DO.

NOW THAT *SHARD* IS THE MOST *DANGEROUS* THING ON THIS PLANET.

WHO'S GOING TO HELP ME *DESTROY* IT?

WE'RE WASTING TIME. LET'S DO THIS.

YOU FIRST.

Psh.

STUPID BOYS.

GREG PAK writer JAE LEE BEN OLIVER artists JUNE CHUNG DANIEL BROWN colorists cover by JAE LEE with JUNE CHUNG

Which makes the current situation even more... annoying.

We're on another world-- with another me and another him...

...and a *superweapon* powered by a *magic crystal* that a self-described trickster goddess says will either *save* or *destroy* our worlds.

I won't lie. I've barely wrapped my head around half of this.

SLADE! FIRE IT UP!

YES, SIR!

But now it's time for *action*.

PARDON.

And the other me steps right up before I have a chance to blink.

SKRRAKK

AGH!

DUCK.

FTOOM FTOOM FTOOM

Eh?

I DON'T THINK I'D STARTED INURING MYSELF TO PUFFERFISH PARALYSIS TOXIN AT YOUR AGE.

THIPP

THIPP

THIPP

UNNNGH

FIRE AT WILLLLLL...

WOW.

NOW IF YOU FELLAS DON'T MIND STEPPING ASIDE...

Our doubles are older. More skilled, more confident.

They treat us like kids.

And I don't like it.

And I don't like it.

Time's short. I could just backhand *Young Me* into the stratosphere.

But I don't know how the crystal would respond.

The boy should *understand* the danger. He's not an idiot.

But I know that pig-headed look. So I just say...

WHAT'S ON YOUR MIND, SON?

I KNOW.

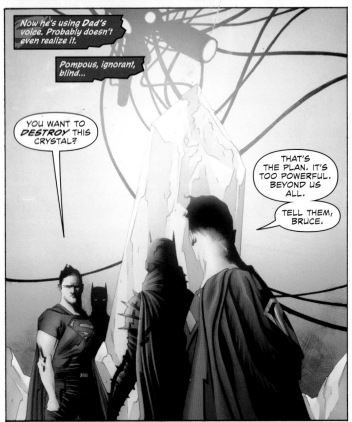

Now he's using *Dad's* voice. Probably doesn't even realize it.

Pompous, ignorant, blind...

YOU WANT TO *DESTROY* THIS CRYSTAL?

THAT'S THE PLAN. IT'S TOO POWERFUL. BEYOND US ALL.

TELL THEM, BRUCE.

IT *MAGNIFIES ENERGY* LIKE NOTHING ELSE IN THE UNIVERSE. AT A CERTAIN POINT, IT *DEFIES PHYSICS.*

IT'S *MAGIC.*

I HATE MAGIC.

AND THE MILITARY'S RIGGED IT UP AS A *WEAPON.*

LIKE CLARK SAID...IT'S JUST TOO *DANGEROUS.*

BUT THE *GODDESS* SAID WE'D NEED IT TO DEFEAT THIS *DARKSEID.*

SHE SAID OUR WORLDS COULD BE *DESTROYED.*

IF YOU DON'T WANT THE CRYSTAL, GIVE IT TO US. WE'LL TAKE IT BACK TO OUR WORLD.

RELAX. YOU CAN HANDLE WHATEVER'S COMING WITHOUT IT.

YOUR *FRIEND* THERE. *YOU'VE* GOT A *SUPERMAN,* TOO.

Psh.

WHAT'S *THAT* SUPPOSED TO MEAN?

SORRY.

SHAKOOM

UKKK!

NNNGH!

CLARK. STOP. OPEN YOUR EARS. THIS CRYSTAL CAN LITERALLY DO *ANYTHING.* IN THE WRONG HANDS--

YOU--

--YOU JUST WANT TO BE THE MOST POWERFUL THING ON THE PLANET.

THINGS... USUALLY WORK OUT *BETTER* THAT WAY.

Y--YOUR W--*WORLD* DOESN'T SEEM TO AGREE.

YOU PUT ON A NICE SHOW BEFORE. BUT LOOK AT THESE *SOLDIERS.* THIS WHOLE *FACILITY.*

THEY MADE THIS WEAPON TO USE AGAINST *YOU.* AND WHY SHOULDN'T THEY?

WHAT HAPPENS WHEN YOU *LOSE CONTROL?*

WHAT'S GOING TO *STOP* YOU?

I'm not dumb. I know Wayne is talking about me, too.

He'll probably kill me someday.

But like the old me says...

...we'll take care of the next threat when it comes.

HIDING IN A BUNKER, *huh*, BOYS?

KINKY.

WAIT, SELINA! LOOK DOWN THERE! IT'S THAT *DEMON!*

"I *HATE* THAT DEMON!"

"*REALLY?* SHE KIND OF LOOKS LIKE *FUN.*"

KAIYO, CHAOS BRINGER! YOU SAY YOU'RE A *GOD?*

STAND AND *FIGHT* LIKE ONE!

AH, BUT THAT WOULD BE PLAYING *FAIR.*

"SHE *POSSESSED* ME. DO YOU HAVE ANY IDEA HOW *CREEPY* THAT IS?"

"YOU GOTTA *LOOSEN UP* A LITTLE, LOIS. LIFE'S MORE *FUN* IF--"

CAREFUL! THAT'S THE *MISSILE LAUNCHER.*

PERFECT!

LOIS... *DIANA* MIGHT NOT BE TOO HAPPY ABOUT GETTING BLOWN UP ALONG WITH--

HA! NOW WHO'S UPTIGHT?

"SHE'LL BE *FINE.*"

GRRR...

SMALLVILLE, KANSAS. EARTH 2.

SMALLVILLE, KANSAS. OUR WORLD.

WORLDS COLLIDE.

SKRRAAKKK

GAH!

KOOOOM

AAAAAAGH!

KENT! HE'S KILLING YOUR **DOUBLE!**

WE'VE GOT TO BREAK THROUGH THIS **SHIELDING!**

NO!

YOU'VE GOT NO CHANCE AGAINST THAT KIND OF POWER--

"--YOU'VE GOT TO SAVE **LOIS!**"

SKKRAK

OH, DAMN.

At the edge of the stratosphere now...

...dying.

They imagined a *Superman-killing* machine, and the crystal *gave* it to them.

CAN YOU HEAR ME, CLARK?

But I always knew you'd be with me at the *end*, Bruce...

Even better...

...I knew you'd have a *plan*.

IT'S EXPERIMENTAL WAYNETECH. CAN'T *ABSORB* THIS ATTACK...

...BUT IT USES TERRILL CONVERSION CELLS TO *REFRACT* ENERGY OF ALL KINDS...

I feel three tendons actually snap in my left shoulder.

But I've got this.

Lois doesn't scream. She just whispers.

Three words. So quietly, she knows only I can hear her.

And my heart breaks and explodes in the same instant.

KENT, WHERE ARE YOU GOING? THE *SHARD*--

DAMMIT.

LOIS IS IN THAT JET. AND *CATWOMAN.*

GO!

WAYNE

I've never jumped this far.

AAAAAGH!

Every muscle feels like it's about to pop.

CLARK! HURRY!

And then I realize I have no idea what I'm doing.

I CAN'T-- I CAN'T CHANGE THE *TRAJECTORY!*

All this stupid power and all I can do is watch them die...

And then Wayne's in my ear.

YOU'VE GOT TO *FLY,* KENT!

FLY? YOU DUMMY. YOU JUST SAID IT YOURSELF. I CAN'T--

YOU'RE *SUPERMAN,* DAMMIT!

WHAT DID I MISS?

COME ON, DEMON! *FIGHT!*

YOU DESTROYED THE *CHAOS SHARD.*

WE'RE DONE HERE.

NOT FOR YOU TO DECIDE.

HA. YOU DON'T UNDERSTAND.

THIS WAS A *CONTEST...*

...TO DETERMINE WHICH OF YOUR WORLDS HAS THE BEST *CHAMPIONS.*

WELL, CLEARLY THAT'S *THIS* WORLD.

NO OFFENSE, KID.

NONE TAKEN.

SO WHAT'D WE WIN?

NOTHING. YOU *LOST.*

WHAT?

I TOLD YOU BEFORE, *LORD DARKSEID* IS COMING. AND YOU *DESTROYED* THE SHARD. YOU'LL *NEVER* BE READY.

BUT *THESE* BOYS...

...THEY *WANTED* THE POWER.

THEY'RE RUTHLESS. RAW. DANGEROUS.

THEY'RE GOING TO *LIVE.* AND SAFE IN THEIR WORLD, *I'LL* LIVE, *TOO.*

DON'T RECALL EXTENDING THE INVITATION--

BOOOOOOOOM

CLARK, YOU'RE NOT EATING.

I'M... I'M SORRY.

I'M SO SORRY.

WHAT ARE YOU *TALKING* ABOUT, CLARK?

I.... DON'T KNOW.

THAT WAS... VERY NICE, BRUCE.

YEAH. SUDDENLY HAD THE FEELING...THAT LIFE IS *SHORT*.

BUT THE NIGHT IS *LONG*.

HA.

Huh.

--MYSTERIOUS DEATHS WERE APPARENTLY CAUSED BY EXPERIMENTAL ROBOTS CREATED BY NOW-FIRED WAYNTECH BOARD MEMBER RALPH MANGUBAT.

Huh.

METRO NEWS
SPECIAL REPORT

GREG PAK writer PAULO SIQUEIRA NETHO DIAZ artists HI-FI colorist cover by IVAN REIS, JOE PRADO & ALEX SINCLAIR
DARKSEID created by JACK KIRBY

THE MORTALS IN
THEIR DIRTY FIELDS
SCREAMED.

AND THE OLD
GODS LAUGHED.

AND LAUGHED.

AND LAUGHED.

...AND STARED DOWN ON THE GREAT CREATORS AND DESTROYERS OF ALL HE KNEW.

NO ONE KNOWS WHAT GAVE HIM THE POWER.

BUT WHEN THE GODS SLEEP...

...NATURE SOMETIMES PRODUCES A SPORT.

EVERY WORLD HAS ONE.

THE SNAKE.

THE BEAST.

THE TRICKSTER...

...PLANTING DOUBT AND HATE IN EVEN THE PUREST SOULS.

AND THEN...

...APOKOLIPS.

WHERE LAUGHTER HAS BEEN BRED OUT OF THE SPECIES.

WHERE EVERY SOUL SILENTLY MARCHES IN STEP.

WHERE EVERYONE FEEDS THE MACHINE.

BUT EVEN HERE...

...NATURE OCCASIONALLY PRODUCES A *SPORT*.

MY NAME IS *KAIYO*.

THE *CHAOS BRINGER*.

AND I'M *BORED*.

BATMAN/SUPERMAN 1
SUPERMAN VARIANT COVER BY GUILLEM MARCH

INSIDE BATMAN/SUPERMAN

PENCILS BY JAE LEE, ORIGINAL SCRIPT BY GREG PAK, COMMENTARY BY GREG PAK, JAE LEE, EDDIE BERGANZA AND RICKEY PURDIN

GP: *People often ask me what it's like working with artist Jae Lee. The answer is pretty simple: Awesome.*

The moody, evocative, elegant, atmospheric worlds Jae Lee and colorist June Chung create stand out from everything else on the stands. Last year, a cinematographer friend who never retweets my comics posts on Twitter instantly shared the first Lee/Chung BATMAN/SUPERMAN pages I posted. The pages have such graphic power and emotional undercurrent, it's impossible not to stare.

What I particularly love about working with Jae is that he's got a brilliant intellectual reason for his bold designs and layouts, but he always brings out the subtle emotion of a scene. To give you a sense of how we work together, please read on for some script excerpts and the pencils that Jae came up with in response.

RP: *The main goal in starting this series was to give readers something they haven't seen before from a Superman/Batman team-up. So pairing Greg's exuberant, emotional writing style with Jae's grounded, cinematic art was what we really needed to make this series a standout. There's no other book like this on the stands, and that's because of Greg and Jae.*

BATMAN/SUPERMAN #1
2013.03.06 - By Greg Pak

PAGE ONE
Panel 1: Gotham City. Beautiful, eerie, and dangerous. We descend through the smog and the dark spires.

LETTERING NOTE: Let's be sure to make Clark's and Bruce's captions distinct. In Jeph's SUPERMAN/BATMAN, they used yellow for Clark and blue for Bruce. I'm wondering if blue for Clark and gray for Bruce might make more sense for us? (We'll also need a variation for next issue if/when we do internal voices for the Earth 2 Batman and Superman.)

1. CLARK'S VOICE (in a caption): My pa always warned me about **Gotham City**.

Panel 2: CLARK KENT, former farm boy and current reporter for the Metropolis Daily Star, walks down the street in the East End, Gotham's worst neighborhood. This is a young Clark, from the time of Morrison's ACTION #1. Big and rumpled, wearing glasses, satchel slung over one shoulder. He's not as beefy as the traditional, fully grown Superman, but he's tall and broad shouldered. He's out of his element, warily/nervously eyeing his surroundings. (And yes, that's partly a put-on — he's in character as Clark. But he's also that hick farmboy, deep inside.) He's glancing over his shoulder — various thugs, hustlers, bums, and shady characters line the streets outside of strip clubs and head shops. (The whole thing's reminiscent of the scene in BATMAN: YEAR ONE when Bruce walks through the East End. Jae, you could even homage that panel directly if you like.)

2. CLARK'S VOICE (in a caption): Growing up on a **farm**, you learn that human beings are **small** and **weak**.

3. CLARK'S VOICE: We only survive by coming together.

4. THUG (to Clark, taunting him): Hey, chicky chicky chicky chicky.

5. WOMAN: Ha ha!

Panel 3: Close on Clark as he turns, eyes sharp, looking towards us. A white rasta DRUG DEALER behind him is murmuring to him. Clark's not looking at the Drug Dealer — he's looking towards us, down the street, as if hearing something no one else can.

6. DRUG DEALER: Bud. Kind bud.

7. CLARK: Uh, no, I'm good, thanks.

8. CLARK'S VOICE: But when people come together in **Gotham**...

Panel 4: In a small, dirty, grassless urban playground, a BIG KID bullies a LITTLE KID, pushing him or smacking him upside the head, while a small pack of kids grin and jeer. It's a multiracial group of kids. The Little Kid, scared but defiant, is in a Muslim American schoolboy's uniform — black vest and tie. There's a scared Muslim girl in school uniform and hijab clutching her bookbag in the background.

9. CLARK'S VOICE: ...the strong just **eat** the **weak**.

10. BIG KID: Where's your camel, Mohammad?

11. LITTLE KID: My name is **Charles**.

PAGE TWO

Panel 1: Sitting on a park bench at the edge of the playground, billionaire BRUCE WAYNE just watches. Bruce is incognito, wearing a leather jacket, boots, and knit cap reminiscent of the clothes he wore during his early training days in BATMAN: YEAR ONE. To a casual observer, he just looks like an idle slacker, slouching, maybe even dozing, hands in pockets. But his eyes are sharp — he's watching the Big Kid knock the Little Kid down.

1. BRUCE'S VOICE: My father was a **doctor**.

2. BRUCE'S VOICE: He saw hundreds of people **cut open** and **shot apart**.

3. BRUCE'S VOICE: He knew how insane and **cruel** this world is.

4. BRUCE'S VOICE: But he promised to always keep me **safe**.

Panel 2: Bruce's POV. Or maybe we're looking over Bruce's shoulder. The Big Kid catches the Little Kid by the collar, raising his fist, about to pound him, hard. The Little Kid's panicking, scrambling to protect himself, but he's about to get beat down hard. The Muslim girl in the back is screaming.

5. BRUCE'S VOICE: Easier said than done.

6. GIRL: Aaaagh!

Panel 3: Closer. The Little Kid's getting shoved to the ground. But from this angle, we can see him clenching his jaw. Making a fist. Today just might be the day he fights back.

7. BRUCE'S VOICE: But this kid's **tougher** than I was.

8. BRUCE'S VOICE: He's thinking about it now.

9. BRUCE'S VOICE: Seconds away from changing **everything**.

Panel 4: Close on Bruce. Head partially lowered — but he's watching everything. Faint, tight smile on his face.

10. BRUCE (small): **Do** it.

GP: Jae likes what folks in comics call "full script," which means all the action and dialogue is written out and all the action is broken down down page-by-page and panel-by-panel. So for these opening two pages of our run on BATMAN/SUPERMAN, I described all the essential elements on the page, devoting one page to introducing Clark Kent and the other to introducing Bruce Wayne. Clearly, the introductions parallel each other. But Jae took it to the next, brilliant level with that gothic arch panel layout on Page One and the eerie, twisty trees on Page Two. He also smartly ended Page One with a close on Clark to parallel the close on Bruce at the bottom of Page Two. Most people will never consciously notice subtle details like that, but they get under our skin and and make the characters and themes sing.

EB: Agree completely with Greg. From the opening of the first page, you know that you have left the real world behind and entered into something wondrous. This is Jae's vision of Gotham City, and its spires, people and the dark woods from which its Dark Knight waits for a very out-of-place Clark Kent tell you that you are in for something completely different.

RP: Besides steering the mood of the page, elements in Jae's art like the twisty trees go a long way toward adding motion and movement to the panels so nothing feels stiff. It may seem like a small trick, but a lot of thought goes into that level of storytelling.

JL: There is nothing more daunting than the opening sequence. Do a good job here, and you buy yourself some goodwill from the reader. Do a bad job, and you lose them forever. No pressure there.

On the last panel of Page Two, I redrew Bruce Wayne's face so many times, there are ghost images galore on the original art board. June had to clean that up in Photoshop. Then, I redrew the face again after she had inked and colored it. She was a saint having to deal with my OCD. Notice the difference between the pencilled version and the printed final version? No? Neither do I anymore. What a waste of time.

PAGE SIX

Let's treat Pages Six and Seven like a double-page spread. But let's also keep the pages divided in the middle so we have the option of running them as separate pages digitally. Page Four is Clark's perspective — Page Five features parallel panels from Bruce's perspective.

Panel 1: Flashback. Wide. The Kent farmhouse at sunrise. Golden morning light, golden sheaves of wheat in the fields all around the house. There's an apple tree a little ways off in the field — wheat grows around it, but someone has carefully plowed around the tree, allowing it to flourish.

NOTE: Since it'll play again at the end of the issue, let's be sure to make this tree distinctive — I'm thinking a wide apple tree with nice, twisty limbs.

1. BRUCE'S VOICE (in a caption): "...or **wherever** you come from."

2. CLARK'S VOICE: **Smallville**. Name says it all.

3. CLARK'S VOICE: I've got **another** home, too. But let's be **honest**...

Panel 2: Flashback continues. JONATHAN KENT, Clark's adoptive father, and a five-year-old Clark climb up the apple tree. Clark's up front, grinning, out on a limb, reaching towards us; Jonathan's behind him, smiling, keeping his boy safe by holding the back of the overalls.

4. CLARK'S VOICE: ... I'll always be **Jonathan Kent's** boy.

5. PA KENT: Attaboy, Clark!

6. CLARK'S VOICE: He and Ma taught me **everything**.

Panel 3: Flashback. Wider shot. Jonathan is lowering Clark by the back of the overalls from the tree. Clark is holding a kitten, clearly just rescued from the tree, out to LANA LANG, a little girl in blue jeans who stands below them. (And yes, this is the little girl version of the Lana we meet in Morrison's ACTION #15.)

7. CLARK: Here you go, Lana!

8. LANA: Yaaay!

9. KITTEN: Mrow!

Panel 4: Flashback. The car wreck scene from Morrison's ACTION #15 — with Ma and Pa Kent's truck on its side in the middle of the road and their bodies on he road behind it.

10. CLARK'S VOICE: And even the day of the **accident**...

11. CLARK'S VOICE: ...when it felt like my chest might **explode** with grief and break the **planet**...

Panel 5: Back in real time. Close on Clark's chest — showing part of the Superman logo on his T-shirt. This can be very close, almost stylized.

12. CLARK'S VOICE: ...I knew they'd always be with me.

ghost or monster stories. Bruce is about five years old. Snuggling up against his father, lying in the crook of his arm. Safe and secure. Thomas has a kind, patient face.

4. BRUCE'S VOICE: He read to me for an *hour*, every single night.

5. BRUCE'S VOICE: I lay against his chest, felt his deep, calm voice reverberating through my body.

6. BRUCE'S VOICE: He read anything I asked him to, no matter how strange or scary.

7. BRUCE'S VOICE: And he *explained* everything. Answered every question.

8. BRUCE'S VOICE: Made it all make *sense*.

Panel 3: Flashback. Six-year-old Bruce kneels in shock between the bodies of his murdered parents. The classic scenario — beneath the streetlight, outside the theater. Pool of blood. Broken pearls.

9. BRUCE'S VOICE: Until it *didn't*.

Panel 4: Flashback. Six-year-old Bruce, eyes wide and face blank with shock, lies down in the street, curling up in the crook of his dead father's arm. As if silently trying to will his father back to life, bring back that feeling of safety of his father reading to him.

10. BRUCE'S VOICE: That's what Kent can never understand.

11. BRUCE'S VOICE: He wants *answers*.

Panel 5: Back in real time. Close on Bruce's chest. Showing just part of the Batman logo on his uniform. Dark and jagged, almost stylized.

12. BRUCE'S VOICE: But sometimes there *aren't* any.

PAGE SEVEN

Panel 1: Flashback. Wayne Manor at sunset. Lonely and imposing. Red and purple skies.

1. BRUCE'S VOICE: You hear *Bruce Wayne* and you think *Gotham City.* But I didn't see a *skyscraper* 'til I was seven.

2. BRUCE'S VOICE: I grew up in *Wayne Manor*...

3. BRUCE'S VOICE: ...my *father's castle*.

Panel 2: Flashback. Bruce's father, THOMAS WAYNE, lies in bed with him, reading him a bedtime story — the book has a cartoony, scary cover —

JL: I believe this is the first time we've seen Superman and Batman's origins. Eddie and Rickey, can you fact-check that for me?

Greg wrote such a wonderful, emotional scene, I wanted to do his words justice. The scene Greg described where Bruce is curled up in his father's arms is heartbreaking. We've seen these scenes played out hundreds of times, but with just a few words, Greg brought it to a whole new level. The backwards layout of the Batman page would have been completely unreadable had Rob not expertly led the eye with his lettering.

RP: I was super-worried the lettering placements on those pages wouldn't read in the right order for fans because of the non-traditional panel grid Jae chose. I should've just trusted him, cause it turned out great. Go back and compare it to the lettered pages in the issue! It's bonkers...

GP: Again, in the script I described a pair of pages that draw parallels between our central characters. And again, Jae took it to an entirely new level with his design and layout. Just one brilliant bit — he worked in the outlines of the Superman and Batman logos entirely on his own.

EB: Even more so, as fans of these characters, we've seen their origin told so many times, but Jae still found a way to breathe new life into them with style. You almost want to cut this out of the book and create a cool piece of origami.

PAGE ELEVEN

Panel 1: Big splash. Angle on Batman, flanked by a trio of creepy giant androids that have emerged from the closets! These are the androids from Jae's insane cover, with dead eyes and scary claws and plenty of exposed mechanisms and wiring. The androids are serving Batman — he's in the middle, crouching, hands raised in scary grasping gestures — the huge androids on either side of him are lunging forward, mimicking/paralleling his grasping gestures with their huge, claw-like hands — grabbing at Mangubat, who's now firing at them with a gun, and Catwoman, who's vaulting and dodging, but getting grabbed! Batman is in the middle, looking like a grim and terrifying puppetmaster.

1. BRUCE'S VOICE: ...I look like a **villain**.

GP: Just a gorgeous splash page. Also worth noting: I wrote the robots you see here into the script after seeing the incredible robots Jae drew on the cover of issue #1. Sometimes your artist comes up with something awesome you never imagined. It's usually a good idea to jump on those things if you can.

EB: Best part of this book is seeing how Greg and Jae really play off each other and gave life to such creations as these steampunk robos.

JL: I hate drawing Catwoman because of Adam Hughes. I hate his Cover Run art book DC recently put out showcasing his covers. I simply hate it. Makes me sick to look at it. He's up there with the greatest illustrators of a nostalgic era long gone.

BATMAN/SUPERMAN #2

05.09.2013 - by Greg Pak

PAGE THIRTEEN

Panel 1: Ma Kent turns to our world's Superman. Eyes probing, calm. Pa Kent is trying to hold her back.

1. MA KENT: Now come over here where I can see you, young man.

2. PA KENT: Martha...

3. MA KENT: Let go of me, Jonathan.

Panel 2: Angle on OW Superman's blank face as he half-stands and Ma Kent approaches. Ma Kent's fingers touch his cheek.

4. MA KENT: I know you.

5. MA KENT: You're my boy, too, aren't you?

Panel 3: Ma Kent and Superman gaze at each other. But Earth 2 Superman stares at the two of them dubiously. He's not interfering with his mother reaching out to OW Superman yet — but he's close enough to intervene if necessary.

5. E2 SUPERMAN: Ma... I'm not so sure —

6. MA KENT: Hush, Clark.

7. E2 SUPERMAN: I was never that **wild**. Never so out of **control**.

Panel 4: OW Superman's POV. Ma Kent's thoughtful, kind face. She's gazing at him/us. Pa Kent behind Ma Kent. His face is starting to soften, too. He's coming around.

8. MA KENT: Maybe this boy's just **lost** more than you ever did.

9. MA KENT: Tell me... **Clark**...

Panel 5: OW Superman stares at her.

10. MA KENT: ... wherever you come from...

11. MA KENT: ... you lost **us**, didn't you?

Panel 6: Tableau. Wide shot. Superman lowers his head. We can't see his face, but he's sobbing. Ma Kent's hand on his shoulder. This is his Ma. And she understands. E2 Superman and Pa Kent standing off to either side, silent, looking down or off to one side. Maybe Pa Kent's scratching the back of his head.

GP: Jae's never scared to try something bold. And for this deeply emotional page, he went full silhouette, and it totally works.

JL: Greg wrote such a powerful scene here. Even Superman would buckle and fall to his knees in this situation. If I took a straightforward approach to this scene, I thought it would lose its emotional impact. By dropping everything in silhouette, the reader can see the anguish on Superman's face better than I could draw it. My drawing a close-up of a tear falling from his eye would be goofy. But if I have his head down and you can't see his face, there's more weight to the scene because you see what you want to see.

EB: An important lesson for all artists: sometimes less is so much more.

BATMAN/SUPERMAN #3
07.01.2013 - by Greg Pak

PAGE TWENTY-ONE

Panel 1: Wonder Woman/Trickster shouts, stretching her arms out. Trickster's ghostly form is partly emerging from Wonder Woman and is kind of superimposed over her.

IMPORTANT: She's wound Wonder Woman's glowing lasso around herself! She speaks the truth!

1. TRICKSTER: The **survival** of your **worlds** hangs in the balance —

2. TRICKSTER: — and all you want to do is **destroy** the weapon that can **save** you?

3. TRICKSTER: **Hear me**, and know that this golden rope compels the **truth**!

Panel 2: Huge panel. Over Trickster's head swirls that horrific, silhouetted vision of Darkseid — slaughtering Supermen and Batmen from other worlds!

4. TRICKSTER: LORD DARKSEID OF APOKOLIPS COMES TO BURN YOUR WORLDS!

5. TRICKSTER: ALL THOSE YOU LOVE WILL DIE!

6. TRICKSTER: AND YOUR OWN SOULS WILL FEED THE FIRE!

Panel 3: Our four heroes squint as blinding white light surrounds them and that boom tube BOOOOM hits the air.

7. SFX: BOOOOOOOOM

8. TRICKSTER: NOW YOU MUST DECIDE —

GP: Here's another example of Jae departing from what the script literally asked for but absolutely nailing the spirit of the moment. This eerie, evocative moment of a stone monster god holding Superman's cape is far more menacing than a straight battle scene would have been.

JL: I could draw Darkseid forever. I love drawing ugly things.

EB: Gotta say we were all eager to see how Darkseid would come into play here. And this would lead to Greg's giving us even more background into the Lord of Apokolips and Kaiyo's role.

RP: Here's a little secret: The design of Kaiyo was actually an unused design we repurposed for use here. The original intent was to use a version of it for the New 52 debut of The Creeper! We went with a different design for him, switched up some things, and used the look here. Note the extra face on the back of her head.

Jae Lee's cover sketches for BATMAN/SUPERMAN #1-4

"Writer Geoff Johns and artist Jim Lee toss you–and their heroes–into the action from the very start and don't put on the brakes. DC's über-creative team craft an inviting world for those who are trying out a comic for the first time. Lee's art is stunning."—USA TODAY

"A fun ride."—IGN

START AT THE BEGINNING!
JUSTICE LEAGUE
VOLUME 1: ORIGIN
GEOFF JOHNS and JIM LEE

JUSTICE LEAGUE VOL. 2: THE VILLAIN'S JOURNEY

JUSTICE LEAGUE VOL. 3: THRONE OF ATLANTIS

JUSTICE LEAGUE OF AMERICA VOL. 1: WORLD'S MOST DANGEROUS

THE NEW 52!

DC COMICS™

JUSTICE LEAGUE
VOLUME 1 ORIGIN

"WRITTEN BY GEOFF JOHNS WITH ART BY THE GODLY JIM LEE, JUSTICE LEAGUE IS A MUST READ."
— COMPLEX MAGAZINE

GEOFF **JOHNS** JIM **LEE** SCOTT **WILLIAMS**